Burning Issues

Pre-Intermediate Level

Shohakusha / Cengage Learning

Burning Issues シリーズの特長と使い方

　この *Burning Issues* シリーズは、「ホットな」（最新であると同時に、人々が熱く語り合って物議をかもすような）題材で定評のある Hot Topics（Cengage Learning 刊）シリーズの日本版です。Hot Topics シリーズの良さはそのまま保ちながら、日本の大学生がより使いやすいよう、テキスト本文の長さを調整し、タスクを日本の大学生にとってよりふさわしいものに作り変えたものです。

Reading 1 & Reading 2 (& Reading 3)

　Hot Topics シリーズの特長のひとつとして立体的な本文構成があります。ひとつのUnitに、テーマは共通でありながら別々の視点から書かれた、あるいはジャンル、文体の異なる2〜4つの本文が配されており、複眼的な思考を可能にしてくれるのです。この *Burning Issues* シリーズもこの構成を踏襲しました。ただし、*Burning Issues* では一つのUnitに含まれる本文を原則としてReading 1 と Reading 2 の二つのみとし、かつこのPre-Intermediate LevelではどのUnitも複数のテキストの合計分量が約300〜350語になるように調整してあります。トピックの関連する本文を複数読むことにより、テーマについての理解が深まると同時に、より様々な表現に出会うことができます。

Outline Reproduction

　選択肢を選ぶことで本文内容を確認してから、その内容を英語で言う練習をするためのタスクです。正しい選択肢を選んですべての文を続けて言えば、それがそのまま本文全体の要約になるように構成してあります。またペアワークとしても使えますので、積極的にスピーキングの練習をしてみましょう。正解を見つけるのは難しくないタスクですが、正解を選ぶのはあくまで出発点であり、その後、その文がスラスラ言えるようになるまで練習するのが主眼です。

Reading-based Writing

　与えられた日本語に合う英文を本文中から探して書き写し、最終的には日本語だけを聞いてその英文を言えるようにするためのタスクです。Outline Reproductionと同様、正解を見つけるのはそう難しいことではありません。しかしやはりそれは単なる出発点です。正解の英文を何も見ずにスラスラ言える・書けるように練習するのが目的です。

Speeded Vocab Production

　英語の語彙を想起する速度をアップするためのタスクです。「語彙力」には、どれだけの数の単語を知っているかという「語彙の広さ」、ひとつひとつの単語の意味や用法をどれだけ知っているかという「語彙の深さ」、そして知っている単語をどれだけ素早く想起して使えるかという「語彙アクセス速度」があります。このタスクは語彙の広さとアクセス速度を増すのが目的です。語彙アクセス速度の向上は英語が実際に使えるようになるための鍵なのです。

Definition-based Vocab Work

　英語の定義を読み、それに相当する単語を選ぶタスクです。ある語の日本語訳に加えて英語定義を知ることで「語彙力」の中の「語彙の深さ」を増すのも目的ですが、それだけではありません。日本語訳をすでに知っている語の英語定義を読むことで、「英語を別の英語で表現する」ことに慣れ、大げさに言えば少しずつ「英語で考える」ことができるようになることを目的としています。最終的には、目標語とその定義を何も見ずに言えるようになるまで練習しましょう。

Idea Exchange

　Reading 1 および Reading 2（& Reading 3）で読んだ内容について、あるいは読むことで触発されて考えたことについて、自分の英語で語る／書くためのタスクです。Reading 1 と Reading 2（& Reading 3）に関連して、読者自身の感じ方や考え方を問う質問を様々な角度から投げかけています。これらの質問に対してまずは答えを頭の中で考えてみるだけでも大いに勉強になるでしょう。質問のなかからいくつか選んで自分なりの答えをまとまった英文（まずは50語程度から始めましょう）で書いてみるのもよいことです。また書いたことは口に出して言ってみましょう。クラスメートと英語で意見の交換をし、質問し合い、感想などを言い合ってみるのも英語運用力の向上に効果的です。

Review Unit

　学習した言語材料の定着のためには意味の分かった語彙、表現、英文に繰り返し触れることが不可欠です。この Pre-Intermediate Level では15番目の Unit として Review Unit を設定し、それまでのユニットの総復習をすることで、より学習効果を高めることを狙っています。まず Definition-based Vocab Work で扱った語の定義を、すべての Unit からランダムに選択肢なしで提示しています。次に Speeded Vocab Production で扱った語の訳語のみを提示しています。いずれも力試しに、また忘れていた語の再確認に利用してください。次に Invisible-gap Filling（空所の見えない空所補充）として、それまでにどこかの Unit で触れた英文を、1語削除した状態で提示しています。文の意味と構造が両方わかっていれば、どこからどのような語が削除されているかが分かるようになっています。こちらは自分の英文理解度のチェックに、また理解度の向上に役立ててください。

　この *Burning Issues* シリーズは、洋の東西を問わず、人間が人間である限り、時代を超えていつまでも話題になり、論議を呼び、深く考えさせられるようなトピックばかりを扱っています。このシリーズを使って学習するみなさんが、我々の生きる社会や人間という存在に関しての考察を深め、自らの考えを進化かつ深化させながら、現代を生き抜くのに不可欠な英語運用能力を高めてくださることを心から願っています。

編著者

Contents

Unit 1
Pampered Pets: Love me? Love my dog! 1
- Reading 1 : New Restaurant with That Special Dog in Mind
- Reading 2 : Life after Death?

Unit 2
Las Vegas: Sin City 7
- Reading 1 : The Tiny White Wedding Chapel: Where Dreams Come True
- Reading 2 : The Lives of Vegas Strippers

Unit 3
The Homeless: It's not their choice 13
- Reading 1 : Homeless to Harvard
- Reading 2 : Let's Help, Not Hurt the Homeless

Unit 4
Sports Doping: Does it matter if you win or lose? 19
- Reading 1 : The Problem of Sports Doping
- Reading 2 : The Real Danger of Sports Doping

Unit 5
Get-Rich-Quick Scams: I've got a deal for YOU! 25
- Reading 1 : Your Door to Wealth and Happiness!
- Reading 2 : Doing Good for Others: Making Money for Yourself

Unit 6
Modern Marriage: Until death do us part? 31
- Reading 1 : Divorce: A Fifty-Fifty Chance?
- Reading 2 : The Government Department of Dating and Marriage?

Unit 7
Beauty Contests: The business of beauty 37
- Reading 1 : Pretty Babies
- Reading 2 : Male Beauty

Unit 8
Gluttony: You are what you eat! 43
- Reading 1 : The Hows and Whys of Gluttony
- Reading 2 : Underfed and Overfed

Unit 9
Shopping: The new drug of choice 49
- *Reading* **1** : Palm Desert Mall: Where Dreams Come True!
- *Reading* **2** : A Personal Reflection on Consumerism

Unit 10
Silly Sports: Can you really call this a sport? 55
- *Reading* **1** : Extreme Ironing
- *Reading* **2** : Eating to Live
- *Reading* **3** : What Makes a Sport?

Unit 11
Shoplifting: Why is the price tag still on your hat? 61
- *Reading* **1** : Different Types of Shoplifters
- *Reading* **2** : Holiday Stress Is Worse for Kleptomaniacs

Unit 12
Drug Trends: Legal but lethal 67
- *Reading* **1** : Legal Drugs and Teenagers
- *Reading* **2** : The World's Most Popular Drug

Unit 13
Nature: Paradise lost—Can we get it back? 73
- *Reading* **1** : The Story of Bikini
- *Reading* **2** : Here Today, Gone Tomorrow

Unit 14
White-Collar Crime: When *A LOT* just isn't enough! 79
- *Reading* **1** : What Is White-Collar Crime?
- *Reading* **2** : What Do White-Collar Criminals Do?

Unit 15
Vocabulary & Sentence Structure Review 85

Hot Topics 1
Copyright © 2006 Heinle, a part of Cengage Learning

This authorized adaptation was published by Shohakusha 2015.
ALL RIGHTS RESERVED. No parts of this book may be reproduced or transmitted in any form or by any means, electronic or mechanical, including photocopying, recording, or any information storage and retrieval system, without permission in writing from the Publisher.

CENGAGE Learning™ CENGAGE™ Learning logo is a trademark under license.

Unit 1
Pampered Pets

Love me? Love my dog!

Reading 1 New Restaurant with That Special Dog in Mind

Do you want to get your dog a special birthday present? If you live in Chicago, you can take Spike or Fifi out to dinner at the Pet Café. It has tables for the humans and eating stands for the dogs. A meal costs less than four dollars. For that price, your dog gets a fortune dog biscuit, and a
05 bowl of peanut-butter-flavored ice cream.

Though some people say, "Dog restaurants are absurd," dog owner Sherry Evans doesn't agree. She went to the Pet Café with her dog, Lulu. "No, it's not ridiculous," she says. "Everyone has to feel needed. Lulu is my sweet, precious baby."   (107 words)

Reading 2 Life after Death?

Kittens Bella and Lucy look alike, but they aren't twins. They're clones. They were created in a laboratory by a company called Genetic Savings and Clone. The company expects to make a lot of money cloning pets after they die. Lou Hawthorne, the president of the company, says,
05 "It's a multibillion-dollar business waiting to happen." Hawthorne's company already has a list of people who want cloned cats. They will each pay $50,000. Dogs will cost more.

One woman has ordered a clone of her late cat. "I made the decision to clone him before he died," Marsha Brooks says. For many people, losing
10 a beloved pet is very upsetting. But even some pet lovers say that cloning seems absurd. However, this cat owner doesn't agree. She wants her cat back. "He was more intelligent than most of the people I know," she said.

But while one woman waits for a clone, others are looking for new pets. Karen and Michael Lawrence decided to spend $50 instead of
15 $50,000. When their cat, Marshall, died, they went to the animal shelter. "You know, there are a lot of great cats and dogs who don't have homes," said Karen.   (198 words)

Outline Reproduction

(a) まず英文の内容に合う選択肢を選び、音声で正解を確認しましょう。
(b) スラッシュ（/）で区切られたチャンク毎に覚えて言う練習をしましょう。
(c) ペアワーク：AさんがA正答あるいは誤答の選択肢を用いた文を音読し、Bさんはそれを聞いてTrueかFalseかを言いましょう。

Reading ①

1. The Pet Café is a restaurant / where you can take your [(A) dogs   (B) cats] for dinner.
2. At the Café, / your dog will get a biscuit and ice cream / for less than [(A) three   (B) four] dollars.
3. Dog owner Sherry Evans believes / that restaurants for dogs are a [(A) ridiculous   (B) good] idea.

Reading ②

1. Genetic Savings and Clone / is a company that clones [(A) cats and dogs   (B) pet owners].
2. Cloning dogs is [(A) more   (B) less] expensive than cloning cats.
3. Some people choose to look for new pets / at [(A) laboratories   (B) animal shelters].

Reading-based Writing

(a) 本文の表現を使って次の日本語を英語にしましょう。
(b) 音声で正解を確認したら音読しましょう。
(c) ペアワーク：Aさんが日本語を読み、Bさんは何も見ずに英語を言いましょう。

Reading ①

(1) 一回の食事の費用は4ドル以下です。

　　A meal _____.

(2) 誰でも必要とされていると感じねばならない。

　　Everyone _____.

(3) イヌのレストランなんて馬鹿げていると言う人もいる。

　　Some people _____.

Reading ②

(4) クローンは実験室で造られる。

　　Clones _____.

(5) その会社はペットの死後、そのクローンを造ることで多くの利益を期待している。

　　The company _____.

(6) 家がないすばらしいイヌやネコはたくさんいる。

　　There are _____.

Speeded Vocab Production ☞

(a) 英単語を音声の後について発音してみましょう。
(b) 日本語だけを見ながら、すべての英単語が30秒以内（最終的には20秒以内）に言えるよう練習しましょう。
(c) ペアワーク：Aさんが日本語をランダムな順番で読み、Bさんは英語を即座に言いましょう。

Xの味付けをした	大切な	クローン	遺伝子の	最愛の
ばかげた	同じに	創りだす	最近亡くなった	気持ちを動転させるような
ばかげた	双子	実験室	決定	知的な

X-flavored	precious	clone	genetic	beloved
absurd	alike	create	late	upsetting
ridiculous	twins	laboratory	decision	intelligent

Definition-based Vocab Work ☞

(a) 上の語群の中から、次の定義に当たる語を選びましょう。
(b) ペアワーク：Aさんがランダムに定義を読み、Bさんは該当する単語を言いましょう。
(c) ペアワーク：Aさんが単語とその定義を読み、Bさんは何も見ずに繰り返しましょう。

1. [　　　　　] = two children born at the same time to the same mother
2. [　　　　　] = an animal produced from the cells of another animal
3. [　　　　　] = a room or building used for scientific research
4. [　　　　　] = good at learning and understanding about things

Idea Exchange 👉

(a) 下の質問にどう答えるか考えましょう。
(b) ペアワーク：それぞれの質問に対する答えをお互いに紹介しながら、話し合ってみましょう。
(c) 論点をひとつに絞って話して（または書いて）みましょう。

1. Would you take your dog to a restaurant?

2. Would you go to a restaurant that served animals?

3. Would you stay in a hotel that allowed animals?

4. What should people with pets do when they go on a vacation?

5. What do you think of the following? Answer, "I think it's OK" "I'm not sure if it's OK" or "I don't think it's OK."
   - Some people buy their pets expensive food.
   - Some people cook food for their pets.
   - Some people let their pets live in their rooms.
   - Some people let their pets sleep on their beds.
   - Some people buy their pets toys.
   - Some people make their pets wear T-shirts.
   - Some people make their pets wear ribbons.
   - Some people take their pets out for dinner.

6. Think about people you know who have pets. Do you agree with the way they treat them? Why or why not?

Unit 2

Las Vegas

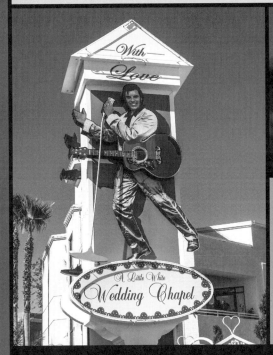

Sin City

Reading 1   The Tiny White Wedding Chapel: Where Dreams Come True

Would you like an unusual wedding quickly? Do you want a memorable event that is also inexpensive? All this is possible! Come see us at the Tiny White Wedding Chapel. We will make your dreams come true. If you want, you can have a simple, candlelit ceremony. But, if you would
05 prefer something unusual or spectacular, we have theater sets, smoke machines, special lighting, and costumes.

One of our most popular weddings is our Elvis Presley package. An Elvis impersonator performs the ceremony and sings some of Presley's hit songs. Or perhaps you would like to get married in another time and
10 place. You can go back to the time of King Arthur or have a wedding in outer space. Remember—the choice is yours. If you can imagine it, we can do it.

(142 words)

Reading 2   The Lives of Vegas Strippers by Karen DiMarco

LAS VEGAS—Being a stripper in Las Vegas has some advantages. The jobs are legal and well paid. Last week, I had a chance to interview Dina, Yolanda, and Sherona—experienced strippers at a club in Las Vegas.

Karen: How did you start working in a strip club, Dina?
05   **Dina**: I was married and working as a waitress. Then my husband took off. I had two kids at home and I needed to make more money.
Karen: What do you think of this job, Sherona?
Sherona: I'm fine. I make good money. Of course, I won't do this forever.
10   I'm studying to be a real estate agent.
Karen: Do some people get good jobs after working as strippers?
Yolanda: Sometimes, but not often. Some get mixed up with drugs and prostitution.
Karen: What about the customers, Yolanda?
15 **Yolanda**: Some of them think that strippers are prostitutes, so they don't understand when we say, "Hands off." But I'm rarely afraid. I wear seven-inch heels, so I'm taller than most of them.

(168 words)

Outline Reproduction 👉

(a) まず英文の内容に合う選択肢を選び、音声で正解を確認しましょう。
(b) スラッシュ（/）で区切られたチャンク毎に覚えて言う練習をしましょう。
(c) ペアワーク：Aさんが正答あるいは誤答の選択肢を用いた文を音読し、Bさんはそれを聞いてTrueかFalseかを言いましょう。

Reading ①

1. The Tiny White Wedding Chapel / are targeting those who want / rather [(A) conventional (B) unusual] weddings.
2. In the Elvis Presley package, / the couple can enjoy / [(A) an Elvis impersonator's performance (B) a movie starring Elvis].
3. In the outer space wedding, / the couple [(A) will actually go to (B) will feel / as if they were in] outer space.

Reading ②

1. In Las Vegas, / stripping is [(A) a legal job (B) an illegal job].
2. In Las Vegas, / strippers [(A) are (B) are not] paid well.
3. [(A) Many (B) Not many] people get good jobs / after working as strippers.

Reading-based Writing 👉

(a) 本文の表現を使って次の日本語を英語にしましょう。
(b) 音声で正解を確認したら音読しましょう。
(c) ペアワーク：Aさんが日本語を読み、Bさんは何も見ずに英語を言いましょう。

Reading ①

(1) 私は普通と違う、安価な結婚式がいい。

　　I would _____.

(2) 私に会いに来れば、あなたの夢を叶えてあげましょう。

　　If _____ , I _____.

(3) 最も人気のあるコメディアンのひとりは、福山雅治のものまねをする人です。

　　One of _____.

Reading ②

(4) 日本で英語が話せるといろいろと有利である。

　　Being _____.

(5) 彼は不動産業者になるために一生懸命勉強している。

　　He is _____.

(6) この仕事は報酬がいいけれど、ずっとやるつもりはないよ。

　　The job _____ , but _____.

Speeded Vocab Production ☞

(a) 英単語を音声の後について発音してみましょう。
(b) 日本語だけを見ながら、すべての英単語が60秒以内（最終的には30秒以内）に言えるよう練習しましょう。
(c) ペアワーク：Aさんが日本語をランダムな順番で読み、Bさんは英語を即座に言いましょう。

思い出に残る	華々しい	合法的な	不動産業者	売春婦
安価な	モノマネ芸人	報酬がよい	～に手を染める	さわるな！
ろうそくに照らされた	大気圏外の宇宙空間	経験豊かな	売春行為	めったに～ない

memorable	spectacular	legal	real estate agent	prostitute
inexpensive	impersonator	well paid	get mixed up with	Hands off!
candlelit	outer space	(a) experienced	prostitution	rarely

Definition-based Vocab Work ☞

(a) 上の語群の中から、次の定義に当たる語を選びましょう。
(b) ペアワーク：Aさんがランダムに定義を読み、Bさんは該当する単語を言いましょう。
(c) ペアワーク：Aさんが単語とその定義を読み、Bさんは何も見ずに繰り返しましょう。

1. [　　　　　] = someone who copies the way other people speak or behave
2. [　　　　　] = allowed by law
3. [　　　　　] = someone whose business is selling houses or land for building

4. [   ] = someone who earns money by having sex with people

Idea Exchange

(a) 下の質問にどう答えるか考えましょう。
(b) ペアワーク：それぞれの質問に対する答えをお互いに紹介しながら、話し合ってみましょう。
(c) 論点をひとつに絞って話して（または書いて）みましょう。

1. Would you like to visit Las Vegas for a vacation? Why or why not?

2. Would you like to live in Las Vegas? Why or why not?

3. What do you think of when you hear the name *Las Vegas*? Circle five words you think of. Add any other words that come to mind.
   - gambling
   - religious
   - beautiful
   - art
   - luxury
   - girls
   - weddings
   - modern
   - conservative
   - families
   - cheap
   - sin
   - money
   - tourists
   - magic
   - lawless
   - desert

4. If the Tiny White Wedding Chapel were in Japan, would you like to get married there? If yes, what kind of wedding would you like to order?

Unit 3

The Homeless

It's not their choice

Reading 1 Homeless to Harvard

Film: *Homeless to Harvard*: The Liz Murray Story
Genre: Drama
Directed by: Peter Levin
Produced by: Michael Mahoney
05 **Starring**: Thora Birch, Kelly Lynch, Michael Riley, Robert Bockstael, Aron Tager

The Story

Homeless to Harvard is the amazing true story of Liz Murray. Liz grew up in very difficult circumstances. Her parents were drug addicts. They didn't have jobs. The family got a check from the government every month. However, her parents used a lot of the money to buy drugs. Liz's parents finally divorced. When she was 15, her mother died from AIDS.

Liz refused to go into the child welfare system because she didn't want to live with strangers in a foster family or a group home. Liz and her friend started living on the streets of New York City.

The girls' lives were incredibly difficult. In good weather, they slept in public parks. In bad weather, they slept underground in the subway. They ate from garbage cans and asked strangers for money.

At the same time, Liz realized that another life was possible. She used a friend's address and started classes in a public high school. She took double the normal number of classes, so she finished in two years. She eventually earned a scholarship and, in 2000, she entered Harvard.

(213 words)

Reading 2 Let's Help, Not Hurt the Homeless

The city of San Miguel should be ashamed of itself. Police are now giving tickets for "illegal lodging" to people who sleep outside. Like most cities in the United States, San Miguel does not have enough affordable housing or homeless shelters. Today, the city only has 2,734 emergency and shelter beds. This number is not nearly enough for the 8,000 homeless who sleep outside every night.

No one likes to see the homeless on the street. However, we shouldn't punish people because they have no place to live. We should help them find homes. We ask city officials to focus on positive solutions — increased housing and services that will help people get off the street. These people need a helping hand, not a slap across the face. —The Editor (127 words)

Unit 3 | The Homeless : It's not their choice

Outline Reproduction

(a) まず英文の内容に合う選択肢を選び、音声で正解を確認しましょう。
(b) スラッシュ（／）で区切られたチャンク毎に覚えて言う練習をしましょう。
(c) ペアワーク：Aさんが正答あるいは誤答の選択肢を用いた文を音読し、Bさんはそれを聞いてTrueかFalseかを言いましょう。

Reading ①

1. Liz's parents were drug addicts / who [(A) didn't have any jobs (B) made money by selling drugs].
2. Living on the streets of New York City / was extremely [(A) boring (B) difficult].
3. Liz entered a top university / after experiencing living [(A) on the streets (B) in a foster family].

Reading ②

1. The police have begun to punish homeless people / for [(A) being homeless (B) stealing things].
2. The number of emergency and shelter beds / is much [(A) larger (B) smaller] / than that of the homeless in the city.
3. The writer is urging the city / to [(A) create more homeless shelters (B) arrest homeless people more strictly].

Reading-based Writing

(a) 本文の表現を使って次の日本語を英語にしましょう。
(b) 音声で正解を確認したら音読しましょう。
(c) ペアワーク：Aさんが日本語を読み、Bさんは何も見ずに英語を言いましょう。

Reading ①

(1) その少女は非常に困難な状況で育った。

　　The girl _____.

(2) 彼女らはゴミ箱をあさって食物を得、他人に物乞いをした。

　　They _____.

(3) 彼女は最終的に奨学金を獲得しハーバードに入った。

　　She _____.

15

Reading ②

(4) 市にはホームレス収容施設の数が足りない。

The city _____.

(5) 誰も通りにホームレスがいるのを見たくはない。

No one _____.

(6) 住むところがないことを理由に人を罰すべきではない。

We shouldn't _____.

Speeded Vocab Production

(a) 英単語を音声の後について発音してみましょう。
(b) 日本語だけを見ながら、すべての英単語が60秒以内（最終的には30秒以内）に言えるよう練習しましょう。
(c) ペアワーク：Aさんが日本語をランダムな順番で読み、Bさんは英語を即座に言いましょう。

状況	児童福祉	結局は	手頃な値段の	職員
離婚する	養子を迎えている家族	非合法の	避難所	解決策
拒む	信じがたいほど	寝泊まり	緊急事態	ビンタ

circumstances	child welfare	eventually	affordable	(n) official
(v) divorce	foster family	illegal	shelter	solution
refuse	incredibly	lodging	emergency	(n) slap

Definition-based Vocab Work

(a) 上の語群の中から、次の定義に当たる語を選びましょう。
(b) ペアワーク：Aさんがランダムに定義を読み、Bさんは該当する単語を言いましょう。
(c) ペアワーク：Aさんが単語とその定義を読み、Bさんは何も見ずに繰り返しましょう。

1. [　　　　　] = the conditions of a person's life
2. [　　　　　] = a building that gives a place to stay for people without home
3. [　　　　　] = a sudden serious and dangerous situation
4. [　　　　　] = someone who has power in an organization

Idea Exchange ☞

(a) 下の質問にどう答えるか考えましょう。
(b) ペアワーク：それぞれの質問に対する答えをお互いに紹介しながら、話し合ってみましょう。
(c) 論点をひとつに絞って話して（または書いて）みましょう。

1. Which type of help do you think the following person should get?

   > My name is Maggie. I am 28 years old and I have two children. Sammy is six and Greta is three. We used to live with my boyfriend, Rick. He is Greta's father. He lost his job at the furniture factory and started drinking. When he got drunk, he got really violent and hit me. Finally, I took the children and left. We're living in my car. I can't get a job because I have no child care.

   1) Take the children from their mother and put them in foster care.
   2) Give the family an apartment and find a job for the mother and child care for the children.
   3) Find the father and make him give his family money.

2. Which type of help do you think the following person should get?

   > I am 15 years old. My name is Angela. I ran away from home because of my stepfather. He and I fought constantly. He used to hit me and punish me all the time. My mother tried to stop him, but he didn't listen. Four months ago, I stole some money from him and bought a bus ticket. Life on the street is hard. At first, I begged for money in the bus station, but I couldn't make enough money that way. Now I work for a drug dealer. I have no choice. If I don't sell drugs, I'll have to sell myself.

   1) Put Angela in a foster home.
   2) Put her in a group home with other teenagers.
   3) Send her home if her parents go to a counselor.

3. Which type of help do you think the following person should get?

> I'm Brad. I am 35 years old. I lost my job as a bus driver because I kept missing work. I suffer from depression. Some days I cannot get out of bed. There are drugs for my problem, but I can't afford them. I owe my landlord two months' rent. If I don't pay him, he'll kick me out. I don't know what to do. My ex-wife and my kids live in Florida, but I can't ask them for help.

1) Make him ask his ex-wife and children for help.
2) Pay for his drugs so that he can go to work.
3) Make him live in a group home for the mentally ill.

Unit 4

Sports Doping

Does it matter if you win or lose?

Reading 1 The Problem of Sports Doping

Sports doping is becoming a bigger and bigger problem. More athletes are taking drugs to help their performance. And it's not just professional athletes. Even some teenagers take drugs to help their high school team win "the big game."

Athletes use drugs in a number of different ways. Some take drugs to make themselves stronger and faster. They also use drugs to mask pain, help them relax, or increase their confidence. But they all take drugs for the same reason—to win. For some, winning is more than just a gold medal. A star athlete can earn a lot of money. For others, winning just means bragging rights—they can talk big for a while. So, although athletes know that working hard is the way to win, they also know that drugs can give them a special advantage. Some of them also believe that not taking drugs is a disadvantage.   (153 words)

Below is a list of the most common drugs that athletes use.

> Relaxes athlete: beta-blockers, alcohol
> Stimulates athlete: cocaine, amphetamines, caffeine
> Reduces weight: diuretics
> Hides other drugs: diuretics, epitestosterone
> Increases muscle size: anabolic steroids, insulin, hCG
> Increases blood oxygen: blood doping, EPO

Reading 2 The Real Danger of Sports Doping

Some people ask, "What's wrong with athletes using drugs to help them compete better?" They say, "Even if drugs are dangerous, the athletes choose to take the risk." In other words, athletes have the right to use any drug they want.

There are several problems with this argument. However, the most important one is that doping creates an unfair environment. Imagine that you and I are runners. I take drugs to help me run faster and I win. You think that you must also take drugs to have a fair chance. One can easily see how doping would soon get out of control. If you start doping, I have to find another way to keep my advantage. Perhaps, I will decide to take more drugs. Maybe I will look for different, stronger drugs to give me a better chance. If I do this, you must follow me or lose. Both of us would continue taking greater and greater risks.   (160 words)

Unit 4 | Sports Doping : Does it matter if you win or lose?

Outline Reproduction

(a) まず英文の内容に合う選択肢を選び、音声で正解を確認しましょう。
(b) スラッシュ（/）で区切られたチャンク毎に覚えて言う練習をしましょう。
(c) ペアワーク：Aさんが正答あるいは誤答の選択肢を用いた文を音読し、Bさんはそれを聞いてTrueかFalseかを言いましょう。

Reading 1

1. Sports doping is becoming a bigger problem / among [(A) professional athletes but not among amateur athletes   (B) both professional and amateur athletes].
2. What each drug does to the athlete's body / [(A) varies   (B) is the same].
3. Many athletes believe / that using drugs will give them [(A) an advantage   (B) a disadvantage].

Reading 2

1. Some people are not convinced / that drugs [(A) are dangerous   (B) should be banned].
2. The biggest problem with doping / is that it creates [(A) a fair playing field   (B) an unfair situation].
3. Once doping is started, / it is [(A) difficult   (B) easy] to break the vicious circle.

Reading-based Writing

(a) 本文の表現を使って次の日本語を英語にしましょう。
(b) 音声で正解を確認したら音読しましょう。
(c) ペアワーク：Aさんが日本語を読み、Bさんは何も見ずに英語を言いましょう。

Reading 1

(1) スポーツのドーピングはますます大きな問題になりつつある。

　　Sports doping _____.

(2) 薬物を使えば特別に有利になることをアスリートは知っている。

　　Athletes _____.

(3) 薬物を使わないと不利になると信じている人もいる。

　　Some believe _____.

21

Reading ②

(4) より良く競うために薬物を使うことの何が悪いのか？

What's _____?

(5) アスリートは自分が使いたいどんな薬物でも使う権利がある。

Athletes _____.

(6) この主張にはいくつかの問題点がある。

There are _____.

Speeded Vocab Production ☞

(a) 英単語を音声の後について発音してみましょう。
(b) 日本語だけを見ながら、すべての英単語が60秒以内（最終的には30秒以内）に言えるよう練習しましょう。
(c) ペアワーク：Aさんが日本語をランダムな順番で読み、Bさんは英語を即座に言いましょう。

成果	自慢する	不利であること	酸素	公平な機会
覆い隠す	得意そうに話す	刺激する	主張	統制が効かなくなる
自信	有利であること	減少させる	環境	続ける

performance	brag	disadvantage	oxygen	a fair chance
(v) mask	talk big	stimulate	argument	get out of control
confidence	advantage	reduce	environment	continue

Definition-based Vocab Work ☞

(a) 上の語群の中から、次の定義に当たる語を選びましょう。
(b) ペアワーク：Aさんがランダムに定義を読み、Bさんは該当する単語を言いましょう。
(c) ペアワーク：Aさんが単語とその定義を読み、Bさんは何も見ずに繰り返しましょう。

1. [   ] = the feeling that you have a high ability
2. [   ] = a thing that helps you to be better than other people
3. [   ] = a gas that is in the air and is necessary for us to live
4. [   ] = a reason somebody uses to show something is true

Idea Exchange

(a) 下の質問にどう答えるか考えましょう。
(b) ペアワーク：それぞれの質問に対する答えをお互いに紹介しながら、話し合ってみましょう。
(c) 論点をひとつに絞って話して（または書いて）みましょう。

1. Do you think sports doping is a problem? Why or why not?

2. How often do you think professional athletes win because of drugs?

3. In what sports do you think professional athletes often or sometimes win because of drugs?

4. What sports do you think are generally "clean" — free from doping?

5. Which statement do you agree with? Why?
   A. "It's not whether you win or lose. It's how you play the game."
   B. "Winning is everything and the only thing."

6. You are a university football player. You work really hard and practice more than your friends, but you rarely play in games. The coach says you run and catch the ball really well but you are too small. A friend says that you should take steroids. They will help you get bigger and no one tests for drugs at your university. Would you agree to take the drugs? Why or why not?

7. You are an excellent athlete. You have a chance to represent your country in the Olympics. Your coach says your competitors are using banned drugs. He thinks that you should use them too. He says that there is one drug that they can't find in drug tests. Would you agree to take the drugs? Why or why not?

Unit 5

Get-Rich-Quick Scams

I've got a deal for *YOU*!

Reading 1 Your Door to Wealth and Happiness!

Would you like to earn $3,000 to $7,000 a week without doing any work? This is possible if you join our Power Profit Team. On our team, you will learn to use the most powerful automated marketing system in the world. With this system, *anyone* can earn thousands of dollars a week. No matter if you are a student or a housewife. No experience is necessary. Your profit is GUARANTEED. (70 words)

Reading 2 Doing Good for Others: Making Money for Yourself

DALTON RIVER—Suppose you are a woman and a good friend tells you about a new women's group. The purpose of the group is to help other women. You have to give $5,000 to a woman in need. Then in just a few days or maybe a week or two, you'll get $40,000. Doesn't it sound good?

Each group usually consists of 15 women. Although it is called a circle, it is actually a pyramid. There is one woman at the top. There are two under her. Then there are four beneath them and eight at the bottom of the pyramid. The woman at the top gets $40,000 when the bottom level of the pyramid is complete. She then leaves the pyramid, and the group divides itself into two more pyramids. All the members move up one level. Both groups must then find eight new members to complete the bottom level of the two new pyramids.

Of course, it's a scam. What's wrong with the plan? The math doesn't work. If each person must find eight people, then eight cycles requires the participation of more than 2 million people. A few more cycles and the number is greater than the entire population of the world.

Police investigators say that the "women helping women" idea is very powerful. Women think it is safe because they believe women don't hurt other women. Unfortunately, that is not always true. (235 words)

Outline Reproduction

(a) まず英文の内容に合う選択肢を選び、音声で正解を確認しましょう。
(b) スラッシュ（/）で区切られたチャンク毎に覚えて言う練習をしましょう。
(c) ペアワーク：Aさんが正答あるいは誤答の選択肢を用いた文を音読し、Bさんはそれを聞いてTrueかFalseかを言いましょう。

Reading ①

1. This text is urging you / to [(A) join their team   (B) be careful] / and get rich.
2. This text claims / that it is [(A) possible   (B) impossible] / for you to earn / thousands of dollars a week.

Reading ②

1. They say / that in this scheme / you will be able to get / [(A) eight   (B) ten] times more money / than you give.
2. They say / that the purpose of the group / is to help [(A) poor women   (B) homeless men].
3. In each group, / only [(A) the woman at the top   (B) the women at the bottom] / will receive $40,000.
4. Many women are tricked by this scam / because women tend to trust [(A) other women   (B) men].

Reading-based Writing

(a) 本文の表現を使って次の日本語を英語にしましょう。
(b) 音声で正解を確認したら音読しましょう。
(c) ペアワーク：Aさんが日本語を読み、Bさんは何も見ずに英語を言いましょう。

Reading ①

(1) 全然働かずに週に30万円を稼ぐのがどうやって可能だというのか。

　　How _____?

(2) あなたは世界で最も強力なシステムが使えるようになります。

　　You will _____.

(3) この仕事には経験は不要です。

　　No _____.

Reading ②

(4) そのグループの目的は、困窮している人を手助けすることだ。

The _____.

(5) 今ではひとグループは20人で構成されている。

Now _____.

(6) その計画のどこがおかしいのかわからない人がたくさんいた。

Many _____.

Speeded Vocab Production ☞

(a) 英単語を音声の後について発音してみましょう。
(b) 日本語だけを見ながら、すべての英単語が60秒以内(最終的には30秒以内)に言えるよう練習しましょう。
(c) ペアワーク:Aさんが日本語をランダムな順番で読み、Bさんは英語を即座に言いましょう。

利益	目的	団体	詐欺	人口
稼ぐ	困窮している	ピラミッド	参加	捜査員
保証する	~から成っている	完結して	全体の	不幸にして

profit	purpose	(n) circle	scam	population
earn	in need	pyramid	participation	investigator
guarantee	consist of ~	(a) complete	entire	unfortunately

Definition-based Vocab Work ☞

(a) 上の語群の中から、次の定義に当たる語を選びましょう。
(b) ペアワーク:Aさんがランダムに定義を読み、Bさんは該当する単語を言いましょう。
(c) ペアワーク:Aさんが単語とその定義を読み、Bさんは何も見ずに繰り返しましょう。

1. [   ] = what you do something for
2. [   ] = a group of people with the same interests
3. [   ] = all members of a group of people living in a place
4. [   ] = a person who examines crimes

Idea Exchange 👉

(a) 下の質問にどう答えるか考えましょう。
(b) ペアワーク：それぞれの質問に対する答えをお互いに紹介しながら、話し合ってみましょう。
(c) 論点をひとつに絞って話して（または書いて）みましょう。

1. Do you think that people today are more dishonest than people in the past?

2. Which of the followings is (1) expensive to start, (2) easy to start, (3) risky, or (4) safe?
   - Lottery
   - Pyramid scheme
   - Internet deals
   - Stock market
   - Real estate
   - Savings account

3. "People who are stupid enough to believe in get-rich-quick scams *should* lose their money." Do you agree with this statement? Why or why not?

4. "People who want to get rich quick deserve to lose their money. They are lazy and just don't want to work like the rest of us." Do you agree with this statement? Why or why not?

5. "There's nothing wrong with getting rich without working. People who buy stocks are making money and they aren't working. Nobody wants to put them in jail." Do you agree with this statement? Why or why not?

Unit 6

Modern Marriage

Until death do us part?

Reading 1 Divorce: A Fifty-Fifty Chance?

Two researchers at the University of Washington created a mathematical formula that predicts divorce.
How do they do it?
A husband and wife talk about a difficult subject for 15 minutes. The researchers videotape them. In addition, they record physical information such as heart rate. Then the researchers listen to the conversation. They watch the body language and look at the facial reactions. After that, they give the couple positive and negative points.

For example, the couple might talk about mothers-in-law. If the husband says, "Your mother is a lot of trouble," the couple gets two negative points. If the wife rolls her eyes, they get two more negative points. However, if the husband says, "Your mother is a lot of trouble, but sometimes she's funny," then the couple gets one positive point. If he smiles, they get another one. A good marriage has five more positive points than negative points.   (151 words)

Reading 2 The Government Department of Dating and Marriage?

The government of the tiny island nation of Singapore is spending money on marriage. Why is the government in Singapore interested in marriage? The government has noticed that women with college degrees often do not get married. Government officials think it is important for them to get married, so they have started a government dating service.

The Social Development Unit (SDU) organizes parties and trips for single people. It also teaches single people about marriage. The SDU says that 50,000 Singaporeans have met and married through this service.

And what do young Singaporeans think of the government dating services? Some of them are happy with it. Ms. Ralls-Tan says that the SDU helped her get married. She and her husband married two years ago. Today they have a six-month-old child. Others just laugh at it. "Single, desperate, and ugly," says a young woman at a local bar. Another says, "We're adults."   (151 words)

Outline Reproduction

(a) まず英文の内容に合う選択肢を選び、音声で正解を確認しましょう。
(b) スラッシュ（/）で区切られたチャンク毎に覚えて言う練習をしましょう。
(c) ペアワーク：Aさんが正答あるいは誤答の選択肢を用いた文を音読し、Bさんはそれを聞いてTrueかFalseかを言いましょう。

Reading ①

1. The formula predicts / how likely it is / for the couple to get [(A) married   (B) divorced].
2. The data the formula uses / are how the couple deal with / a [(A) happy   (B) difficult] topic.
3. The higher / the points the couple get, / the [(A) more   (B) less] likely it is / for their marriage / to come to an end.

Reading ②

1. The government dating service / is mainly targeting / [(A) educated   (B) uneducated] women.
2. This service provides single people / with chances to [(A) meet / someone new   (B) learn / how to live alone].
3. Some young people laugh at the service / because they feel / the service is treating them / like [(A) adults   (B) children].

Reading-based Writing

(a) 本文の表現を使って次の日本語を英語にしましょう。
(b) 音声で正解を確認したら音読しましょう。
(c) ペアワーク：Aさんが日本語を読み、Bさんは何も見ずに英語を言いましょう。

Reading ①

(1) 研究者たちは離婚を予測する数学的公式を作った。

　　The _____.

(2) その公式は心拍数などの身体的情報を使う。

　　The _____.

(3) 身振りや顔に出る反応から多くのことが分かる。

　　You can _____.

Reading ②

(4) 大卒の資格（学士号）がある女性は結婚しないことがよくある。

Women _____.

(5) 政府は若い人のためのパーティや旅行を企画する。

The _____.

(6) 一部の若者は政府が若者の手助けをして結婚させるという考えを嘲笑する。

Some _____.

Speeded Vocab Production ☞

(a) 英単語を音声の後について発音してみましょう。
(b) 日本語だけを見ながら、すべての英単語が60秒以内（最終的には30秒以内）に言えるよう練習しましょう。
(c) ペアワーク：Aさんが日本語をランダムな順番で読み、Bさんは英語を即座に言いましょう。

公式	研究者	反応	くるくる回す	組織する・企画する
予測する	脈拍数	負の	局、省	必死な
島国	顔の	義理の母親	大卒の資格	発展

formula	researcher	reaction	(v) roll	organize
predict	heart rate	negative	department	desperate
island nation	facial	mother-in-law	college degree	development

Definition-based Vocab Work ☞

(a) 上の語群の中から、次の定義に当たる語を選びましょう。
(b) ペアワーク：Aさんがランダムに定義を読み、Bさんは該当する単語を言いましょう。
(c) ペアワーク：Aさんが単語とその定義を読み、Bさんは何も見ずに繰り返しましょう。

1. [   ] = mathematical relationship expressed in symbols
2. [   ] = someone whose job is to study and investigate a subject
3. [   ] = how fast your heart is beating
4. [   ] = what you do as a result of something that has happened

Idea Exchange

(a) 下の質問にどう答えるか考えましょう。
(b) ペアワーク：それぞれの質問に対する答えをお互いに紹介しながら、話し合ってみましょう。
(c) 論点をひとつに絞って話して（または書いて）みましょう。

1. Are you dating someone now?

2. Do you have a steady boyfriend/girlfriend? If not, are you looking for one?

3. Would you like to get married in the future?

4. Do you think it is OK for women to propose to men? Why or why not?

5. How important is communication in a relationship?

6. Do you think mathematics can predict divorces?

7. In your opinion, which of the following are the five most important elements for a successful marriage?
   - agreement on how to raise children
   - agreement on money issues
   - approval from family members
   - fidelity
   - open communication
   - one decision maker
   - same culture
   - same religion
   - satisfactory sexual relationship
   - shared values
   - similar level of education
   - similar personalities

Unit 7

Beauty Contests

The business of beauty

Reading 1 Pretty Babies

　　Tina Crosby looked confused. This was her first beauty contest and she was nervous. The judge asked her, "How do you relax?" She bravely tried to smile, but she couldn't answer the question. "Ummm. I don't know," was all that she could say.

05　　That's not surprising. Tina is only five years old. She was not well-spoken but she was cute enough to win. A smiling Tina (and her proud mother) went home with a trophy and a "diamond" crown.

　　Beauty contests for very young children are common today. Some child psychologists say that the contests have many more disadvantages
10 than advantages. They think that they teach girls that beauty is very important. Others worry that these children grow up too fast and that can cause psychological problems later on.

　　Baby beauty contests are big business. There are probably about 5,000 beauty pageants in the United States every year. About 25 percent are for
15 children. And the business is growing. There are more and more contests every year.　　　　　　　　　　　　　　　　　　　　　(166 words)

Reading 2 Male Beauty

　　Beauty contests for women are very common. However, most men do not usually have opportunities to win prizes for being handsome. That is because most cultures don't consider a man's appearance as important as a woman's. Men don't have to be handsome, but women are supposed to
05 be beautiful. However, there is one exception—bodybuilding.

　　In bodybuilding contests, men compete for cash prizes and titles such as Mr. Universe and Mr. America. The contestants stand in front of the judges and the audience. In order to show their muscles, they pose in certain ways. There are competitions for separate parts of the body. One
10 man might have the best back. Another might have the best chest or arms. However, there is also a prize for the best body overall. This man becomes Mr. Universe or Mr. America.　　　　　　　　　　　　(136 words)

Outline Reproduction

(a) まず英文の内容に合う選択肢を選び、音声で正解を確認しましょう。
(b) スラッシュ（ / ）で区切られたチャンク毎に覚えて言う練習をしましょう。
(c) ペアワーク：Aさんが正答あるいは誤答の選択肢を用いた文を音読し、Bさんはそれを聞いてTrueかFalseかを言いましょう。

Reading ①　

1. Tina was a [(A) five-year-old　(B) ten-year-old] / who won a beauty contest / for very young children.
2. Beauty contests communicate to girls / that one's appearance [(A) is very important　(B) does not matter].
3. About one in [(A) three　(B) four] beauty pageants in the States / are for children.

Reading ②　

1. In most cultures, / male beauty is considered / [(A) as important as　(B) less important than] female beauty.
2. Body building contests offer / [(A) both cash and fame　(B) fame but not cash] / to the winner.
3. Mr. Universe is the man / who has [(A) the best body overall　(B) the best-looking face].

Reading-based Writing

(a) 本文の表現を使って次の日本語を英語にしましょう。
(b) 音声で正解を確認したら音読しましょう。
(c) ペアワーク：Aさんが日本語を読み、Bさんは何も見ずに英語を言いましょう。

Reading ①　

(1) 彼女はうまく話せなかったが、優勝するだけの可愛さはあった。

　　She _____.

(2) 非常に幼い子どものための美人コンテストは良い点よりも悪い点のほうがずっと多い。

　　Beauty _____.

(3) 速く成長しすぎると後々心理的な問題を引き起こすことがある。

　　Growing up _____.

Reading ②

(4) ほとんどの男性には顔の良さによって賞を獲得する機会はない。

　　Most _____.

(5) 男性はハンサムでなくてもよいが、女性は美しいものだということになっている。

　　Men _____ , but _____.

(6) ボディビルのコンテストでは、男性たちが賞金とタイトルをかけて競う。

　　In _____ , men _____.

Speeded Vocab Production

(a) 英単語を音声の後について発音してみましょう。
(b) 日本語だけを見ながら、すべての英単語が60秒以内(最終的には30秒以内)に言えるよう練習しましょう。
(c) ペアワーク：Aさんが日本語をランダムな順番で読み、Bさんは英語を即座に言いましょう。

混乱している	心理学者	機会	〜を目指して競う	ポーズを取る
勇敢に	心理的な	外見	出場者	競争
冠、頭飾り	派手なショー	例外	観客	全体的な

confused	psychologist	opportunity	compete (for)	pose
bravely	psychological	appearance	contestant	competition
crown	pageant	exception	audience	overall

Definition-based Vocab Work

(a) 上の語群の中から、次の定義に当たる語を選びましょう。
(b) ペアワーク：Aさんがランダムに定義を読み、Bさんは該当する単語を言いましょう。
(c) ペアワーク：Aさんが単語とその定義を読み、Bさんは何も見ずに繰り返しましょう。

1. [　　　　　] = a circle put on the head of someone who has won a contest
2. [　　　　　] = someone whose job is to research how people think and feel
3. [　　　　　] = someone who has entered a contest
4. [　　　　　] = a group of people watching or listening to a performance

Idea Exchange

(a) 下の質問にどう答えるか考えましょう。
(b) ペアワーク：それぞれの質問に対する答えをお互いに紹介しながら、話し合ってみましょう。
(c) 論点をひとつに絞って話して（または書いて）みましょう。

1. A person who runs children's beauty pageants say, "Being in a beauty contest is the same as playing on a soccer team. It's not about winning." Do you agree or disagree? Why?

2. Why do you think parents enter their children in beauty contests?

3. Would you be in a beauty contest?

4. Would you be a judge in a beauty contest?

5. Would you watch a beauty contests on television?

6. Do you attend beauty contest?

7. Would you encourage a good-looking friend to enter a beauty contest?

8. Would you let your daughter compete in a beauty contest?

9. Would you protest against beauty contests?

10. Should there be beauty contests for women? For men? For children? Why or why not?

Unit 8

Gluttony

You are what you eat!

Reading 1 The Hows and Whys of Gluttony

The dictionary says that a glutton is a person who eats too much. If so, the United States is a nation of gluttons.

We now know that gluttony is not just about being self-indulgent. Being overweight can cause serious health problems such as heart disease, high blood pressure, and diabetes. So, why are so many of us eating ourselves to death?

Experts in obesity research say there are a number of reasons. First, food is cheaper than it was in the past. They say that it is natural to eat when we can. Second, we lead very sedentary lives. Most of us have desk jobs. We don't walk to shops, schools, or banks—we drive cars. Furthermore, at home we have a lot of machines to help us. We don't push lawn mowers—we ride on them. We don't rake leaves—we blow them away with leaf blowers. We don't wash dishes anymore—the dishwasher does. In addition, robot vacuum cleaners clean our floors. We usually call these machines labor-saving devices. Maybe if we called them fat-development devices, people would stop using them.   (177 words)

Reading 2 Underfed and Overfed

The Worldwatch Institute says that the number of overweight people in the world equals the number of underweight people for the first time in history. Today there are about 1.1 billion people who are hungry. There are also about 1.1 billion people who are overweight.

Hunger is decreasing around the world. There are fewer starving people every year. Unfortunately, the number of overweight people is increasing faster than the starvation rate is decreasing. In the United States, 55 percent of adults are overweight; 23 percent of American adults are considered obese.

However, the United States is not alone. Surprisingly, excessive body weight and obesity are increasing rapidly in developing countries, too. The report states that in the past, people in these countries were unhealthy because they did not have enough to eat. Now they are unhealthy because they overeat.   (139 words)

Outline Reproduction

(a) まず英文の内容に合う選択肢を選び、音声で正解を確認しましょう。
(b) スラッシュ（／）で区切られたチャンク毎に覚えて言う練習をしましょう。
(c) ペアワーク：Aさんが正答あるいは誤答の選択肢を用いた文を音読し、Bさんはそれを聞いてTrueかFalseかを言いましょう。

Reading ①

1. The United States is full of people / who eat too [(A) much   (B) little].
2. People who are overweight / are [(A) more   (B) less] likely to have some health problems / than those who are not.
3. One reason for the increase / in the number of obese people / is the increase in the types of [(A) machines   (B) animals] / that work for us.

Reading ②

1. Traditionally, / there have been [(A) more   (B) fewer] overweight people / than underweight people / in the world.
2. It is likely / that in the near future, / there will be [(A) more   (B) fewer] overweight people / than starving people.
3. Obesity is a problem / [(A) in developed countries alone   (B) in developing countries as well].

Reading-based Writing

(a) 本文の表現を使って次の日本語を英語にしましょう。
(b) 音声で正解を確認したら音読しましょう。
(c) ペアワーク：Aさんが日本語を読み、Bさんは何も見ずに英語を言いましょう。

Reading ①

(1) 辞書によれば大食家とは食べ過ぎる人である。

　　The _____.

(2) 太り過ぎは心臓病、高血圧、糖尿病の原因になりうる。

　　Being _____.

(3) これらの機械は省力化装置ではなく、脂肪増大装置と呼ばれるべきだ。

　　These _____.

Reading ②

(4) 世界中の過体重の人の数は過小体重の人の数と等しい。

　　The number _____.

(5) 肥満は発展途上国でも急速に増加している。

　　Obesity _____.

(6) 過去においては、発展途上国の人々は十分な食べ物がないために不健康だった。

　　In the _____ , _____.

Speeded Vocab Production ☞

(a) 英単語を音声の後について発音してみましょう。
(b) 日本語だけを見ながら、すべての英単語が60秒以内（最終的には30秒以内）に言えるよう練習しましょう。
(c) ペアワーク：Aさんが日本語をランダムな順番で読み、Bさんは英語を即座に言いましょう。

血圧	座ってばかりいる	装置	食べ過ぎている	飢えている
糖尿病	芝刈り機	脂肪	研究所	見なされる
肥満した	省力のための	十分に食べていない	～と等しい	過度の

blood pressure	sedentary	device	overfed	(a) starving
diabetes	lawn mower	(n) fat	(n) institute	be considered
obese	labor-saving	underfed	(v) equal	excessive

Definition-based Vocab Work ☞

(a) 上の語群の中から、次の定義に当たる語を選びましょう。
(b) ペアワーク：Aさんがランダムに定義を読み、Bさんは該当する単語を言いましょう。
(c) ペアワーク：Aさんが単語とその定義を読み、Bさんは何も見ずに繰り返しましょう。

1. [　　　　　] = a disease in which there is too much sugar in your blood
2. [　　　　　] = always sitting down and not moving enough
3. [　　　　　] = a machine with blades for cutting grass
4. [　　　　　] = a machine or tool for a specific purpose

Idea Exchange

(a) 下の質問にどう答えるか考えましょう。
(b) ペアワーク：それぞれの質問に対する答えをお互いに紹介しながら、話し合ってみましょう。
(c) 論点をひとつに絞って話して（または書いて）みましょう。

1. Which problem is more serious—starvation or obesity? Why or why not?

2. In what ways could people try to increase their physical activity?

3. In Japan, in what ways do people eat differently that they used to 10 years ago, 30 years ago, and 100 years ago?

4. In Japan there seem to be fewer obese people than there are in the United States. Why is this?

5. Do you think obese people have become obese because of their own fault?

6. How much responsibility does each of the following groups have for the increase in obesity? None? Very little? Some? A lot? Almost all?
   - Individual adults
   - Parents
   - Government
   - Doctors
   - Schools
   - Food manufacturers
   - Advertisers
   - Restaurants

7. What can each of the above groups can do to help people eat healthier food?

8. A university professor proposes that the government should create a special tax on high-calorie foods such as french fries. Do you think it is a good idea? Why or why not?

Unit 9
Shopping

The new drug of choice

Reading 1 Palm Desert Mall: Where Dreams Come True!

Palm Desert Mall is the biggest and the best place to shop in Southern California! It offers visitors true *shoppertainment*. At Palm Desert, stores, entertainment, restaurants and fun are all combined into one. Shoppers say they're addicted to Palm Desert.

Palm Desert Mall has over 250 department stores, specialty shops, restaurants, entertainment venues, and carts and kiosks—all under one roof. And that roof is BIG. It is as large as 43 football fields!

For entertainment, moviegoers can choose from 53 movies! Palm Desert Mall also has many different special events every week. There are concerts, fashion shows, parties, and parades.

There are restaurants for everyone's taste and pocketbook. Palm Desert Mall welcomes millions of visitors each year. Come and see how we can make your dreams come true!   (125 words)

Reading 2 A Personal Reflection on Consumerism By Kathy Fairclough

Imagine that you have a week off from school or work. However, in this week, you cannot spend any money. How would you spend your time? Perhaps you would take a walk on the beach with your best friend. Maybe you would play with your dog. Maybe you would draw a picture or write a story.

On our deathbeds, it is likely that non-consuming experiences like these will be our most important memories. Non-consuming activities are active, and they don't come in a package. You make the experience yourself. However, if you watch a movie with a friend, you will each have a packaged experience, requiring no action and little interaction between the two of you.

The consumerist environment we live in encourages us to have packaged experiences. However, we can start a personal revolution against consumerism. How? By consuming less. We can ask ourselves; what experiences bring us the greatest satisfaction? Then we can organize our lives so that we have more of those kinds of experiences. The capitalist system can use us or we can use it. It's our choice.   (182 words)

Outline Reproduction

(a) まず英文の内容に合う選択肢を選び、音声で正解を確認しましょう。
(b) スラッシュ（ / ）で区切られたチャンク毎に覚えて言う練習をしましょう。
(c) ペアワーク：Aさんが正答あるいは誤答の選択肢を用いた文を音読し、Bさんはそれを聞いてTrueかFalseかを言いましょう。

Reading ①

1. Palm Desert Mall is a place / where you can [(A) shop and eat   (B) shop but not eat].
2. Entertainment at the Mall includes / movies, concerts, fashion shows, / parties, [(A) and parades   (B) but not parades].
3. The brochure says / that you can choose / from [(A) many types of food   (B) only a couple of types of food].

Reading ②

1. Taking a walk on the beach / with your best friend / is one example / of [(A) a consuming experience   (B) a non-consuming experience].
2. Consuming experiences are [(A) passive   (B) active], / and they [(A) come   (B) don't come] in a package.
3. The author urges us to consume [(A) more   (B) less] / and to enjoy more [(A) packaged   (B) non-packaged] experiences.

Reading-based Writing

(a) 本文の表現を使って次の日本語を英語にしましょう。
(b) 音声で正解を確認したら音読しましょう。
(c) ペアワーク：Aさんが日本語を読み、Bさんは何も見ずに英語を言いましょう。

Reading ①

(1) ここは南カリフォルニアで最大で最高の買い物スポットです。

　　This is _____.

(2) レストランは10店舗から選べます。

　　You _____.

(3) あらゆる人の好みと予算にあうレストランがあります。

　　There _____.

Reading ②

(4) 非消費的な経験が最も大切な思い出になるでしょう。

　　Non-consuming _____.

(5) 映画を見ても、見ている人たちの間ではほとんどやりとりをする必要がありません。

　　Watching _____.

(6) 消費を減らすことで、我々は消費主義に反対する個人的革命を始めることができます。

　　We can _____.

Speeded Vocab Production ☞

(a) 英単語を音声の後について発音してみましょう。
(b) 日本語だけを見ながら、すべての英単語が60秒以内（最終的には30秒以内）に言えるよう練習しましょう。
(c) ペアワーク：Aさんが日本語をランダムな順番で読み、Bさんは英語を即座に言いましょう。

やみつきである	金銭状態・資金力	死の床	必要とする	革命
舞台・会	熟考・意見	可能性が高い	やりとり、会話	満足
嗜好・好み	消費者	経験	促す	資本主義のしくみ

be addicted to ~	pocketbook	deathbed	require	revolution
venue	reflection	likely	interaction	satisfaction
(n) taste	consumer	(n) experience	encourage	capitalist system

Definition-based Vocab Work ☞

(a) 上の語群の中から、次の定義に当たる語を選びましょう。
(b) ペアワーク：Aさんがランダムに定義を読み、Bさんは該当する単語を言いましょう。
(c) ペアワーク：Aさんが単語とその定義を読み、Bさんは何も見ずに繰り返しましょう。

1. [　　　　　] = a place where an organized event takes place
2. [　　　　　] = what you like and prefer
3. [　　　　　] = a person who buys things for personal use
4. [　　　　　] = a complete change in ways of thinking or behaving

Idea Exchange 👉

(a) 下の質問にどう答えるか考えましょう。
(b) ペアワーク：それぞれの質問に対する答えをお互いに紹介しながら、話し合ってみましょう。
(a) 論点をひとつに絞って話して（または書いて）みましょう。

1. How often do you window-shop?

2. How often do you go shopping with friends?

3. How often do you go shopping with a family member?

4. How often do you shop on the Internet?

5. When you want to buy a book or books, do you prefer to go to an Internet bookstore like Amazon or do you want to go to a real bookstore in your city? Why?

6. Do you think shopping can be an addiction?

7. Do you have a shopping mall or a department store that you love?

8. How important is shopping in your life?

9. What would you do with your free time if you couldn't go shopping for three months?

Unit 10

Silly Sports

Can you really call this a sport?

Reading 1 Extreme Ironing

What activities are sports? Running and football? Sure. Synchronized swimming? Probably. Ballroom dancing? Maybe. Playing cards? Probably not. Gardening? Definitely not. Most people believe that sports must combine physical activity and competition. If we use this definition, then extreme ironing is a sport.

What is extreme ironing? Extreme ironing is pressing clothes in very difficult places. Ironists must carry their irons, ironing boards, and wrinkled laundry with them to the competition site. The competitors get more points for the difficulty of the location. However, the quality of the ironing is important, too. Each item must be well pressed.   (98 words)

Reading 2 Eating to Live

KENNEBUNK, MAINE— Sonya Thomas of Alexandria, Virginia, finished 38 lobsters in 12 minutes and won the World Lobster-Eating Contest on Saturday. She ate a total of 4.39 kilograms of lobster meat. Sonya won $500 and a trophy.

Sonya has a lot of trophies. She is a professional "gurgitator"— she eats for a living. The International Federation of Competitive Eating (IFOCE) says that Thomas is the best gurgitator in the United States.

(71 words)

Reading 3 What Makes a Sport?

What is a sport? In my opinion, there are some activities that are definitely sports: baseball, football, basketball, hockey, golf, and bowling. And there are some activities that are definitely not sports: cheerleading, dance, figure skating, and gymnastics.

How did I decide? An activity is not a sport if a judge or a group of judges chooses the winner. Judges decide the winners of figure skating, cheerleading, dance, and gymnastics competitions. Therefore, none of them are sports.

In the non-sports listed, judges determine the winners based on their opinions. Maybe they think one competitor wins too often or not enough. Perhaps they don't like one of the contestants. Perhaps they just prefer one competitor's music or their clothes. The point is that we can never be certain that the winner was really the best.   (134 words)

Outline Reproduction

(a) まず英文の内容に合う選択肢を選び、音声で正解を確認しましょう。
(b) スラッシュ（/）で区切られたチャンク毎に覚えて言う練習をしましょう。
(c) ペアワーク：Aさんが正答あるいは誤答の選択肢を用いた文を音読し、Bさんはそれを聞いてTrueかFalseかを言いましょう。

Reading ①

1. In extreme ironing, / [(A) both physical activity and competition / take place   (B) neither physical activity nor competition / takes place].
2. Extreme ironing / is ironing [(A) ordinary clothes / in extraordinary places   (B) extraordinary clothes / in ordinary places].
3. Irons, ironing boards, and laundry / [(A) are   (B) are not] provided / by the organizers of the competitions.

Reading ③

1. Activities that are definitely sports / include [(A) baseball, football, and basketball   (B) cheerleading, dance, and figure skating].
2. Activities that are definitely not sports / include [(A) baseball, football, and basketball   (B) cheerleading, dance, and figure skating].
3. According to the author's definition, / an activity [(A) is   (B) is not] a sport / if a judge or a group of judges chooses the winner.

Reading-based Writing

(a) 本文の表現を使って次の日本語を英語にしましょう。
(b) 音声で正解を確認したら音読しましょう。
(c) ペアワーク：Aさんが日本語を読み、Bさんは何も見ずに英語を言いましょう。

Reading ①

(1) ほとんどの人はスポーツには肉体的活動と競争的要素が組み合わさっていなければならないと考えている。

   Most _____.

(2) 彼らは自分のアイロンとアイロン台と洗濯物を持参せねばなりません。

   They _____.

Reading ②

(3) 彼女は合計4.39キロのロブスターの身を食べ、500ドルとトロフィーを獲得した。

   She _____ and _____.

Reading ③

(4) 一部のスポーツでは、審判員が自分の意見で勝者を決める。

In _____ , _____.

(5) フィギュアスケート、チアリーディング、体操競技の勝者は審判員が決める。

Judges _____.

(6) 要点は優勝者が本当にベストだったのだと私たちが確信を持てないということだ。

The point is _____.

Speeded Vocab Production ☞

(a) 英単語を音声の後について発音してみましょう。
(b) 日本語だけを見ながら、すべての英単語が60秒以内（最終的には30秒以内）に言えるよう練習しましょう。
(c) ペアワーク：Aさんが日本語をランダムな順番で読み、Bさんは英語を即座に言いましょう。

タイミングを一致させた	生活のために	シワのよった	連邦・連盟	決める
絶対に	定義	洗濯物	競争的な	意見
組み合わせる	極端な	位置・場所	体操	競技者

synchronized	for a living	wrinkled	federation	determine
definitely	definition	laundry	competitive	opinion
combine	extreme	location	gymnastics	competitor

Definition-based Vocab Work ☞

(a) 上の語群の中から、次の定義に当たる語を選びましょう。
(b) ペアワーク：Aさんがランダムに定義を読み、Bさんは該当する単語を言いましょう。
(c) ペアワーク：Aさんが単語とその定義を読み、Bさんは何も見ずに繰り返しましょう。

1. [　　　　　] = a phrase that says exactly what a word means
2. [　　　　　] = clothes that need to be washed
3. [　　　　　] = two or more groups that have joined together to form a larger group
4. [　　　　　] = your feelings or thoughts about something

Idea Exchange 👉

(a) 下の質問にどう答えるか考えましょう。
(b) ペアワーク：それぞれの質問に対する答えをお互いに紹介しながら、話し合ってみましょう。
(c) 論点をひとつに絞って話して（または書いて）みましょう。

1. What do you think of extreme ironing? Is it a sport? Would you participate in it?

2. What do you think of competitive eating? Is it a sport? Would you participate in it?

3. Are there any sports that you think are silly?

4. Do you think that a sport must have a clear winner? Then, is mountain climbing a sport?

5. Do you agree with the following definition of a sport? Why or why not? "A human activity that is competitive, has a definite result, requires physical activity and physical skill."

6. At present, golf is a sport that does not have judges. Do you think golf should introduce judges?

7. Long jumping is only about distance. However, ski jumping is not only about how far a jumper flies but also about how beautifully the jumper flies and lands. The "style points" are decided by judges. Do you think it is a good system? Or do you think that ski jumping should do away with this "style" element?

Unit 11

Shoplifting

Why is the price tag still on your hat?

Reading 1 Different Types of Shoplifters

Compulsive Shoplifters: 85%
For these people, shoplifting is a compulsion. Usually they steal items that are inexpensive. If they are caught, they might cry and feel shame.
Professionals: 2%
Professional shoplifters steal expensive items. If the police catch them, they will try to run away. If they can't escape, they show no emotion. They never feel guilty.
The Poor: 5%
These shoplifters usually steal necessities like food, baby diapers, toiletries, or children's clothing. If they are caught, they will say that they are sorry. However, they believe shoplifting is necessary to support themselves and their families.
Thrill Seekers: 5%
These shoplifters will often steal in groups. Many teenagers belong to this type. They steal because it's exciting. They often feel afraid if the police catch them.
Drug Addicts: 2%
Like professionals, they take expensive items. Then they sell these things to get money to buy drugs. If they are caught, they will try to run away.
Kleptomaniacs: 1%
Kleptomaniacs are impulsive. They will often take items they don't need and can't use. If they are caught, they will usually admit they are kleptomaniacs. They do not feel guilty and they are not ashamed.

(193 words)

Reading 2 Holiday Stress Is Worse for Kleptomaniacs

Springfield, Ohio; November 28—Although the holidays are stressful for many people, kleptomaniacs have an even greater problem than most of us. They are afraid to go shopping because they have a compulsion to steal. Five years ago, Terry Schulman formed CASA (Cleptomaniacs and Shoplifters Anonymous). He says his own addiction became so bad that he stole something every day. "The addictive-compulsive shoplifter, like myself and most of the people who come to the group, shoplift as a way to cope with life," Schulman says. CASA is a support group. Some people come because a judge has told them that they must. However, most people come because they want to get better. Many people at a recent CASA meeting were worried about the holidays. They said that the stress of the holidays and the need to shop increased the chance that they might steal.

(143 words)

Outline Reproduction

(a) まず英文の内容に合う選択肢を選び、音声で正解を確認しましょう。
(b) スラッシュ（/）で区切られたチャンク毎に覚えて言う練習をしましょう。
(c) ペアワーク：Aさんが正答あるいは誤答の選択肢を用いた文を音読し、Bさんはそれを聞いてTrueかFalseかを言いましょう。

Reading ①

1. [（A）Compulsive　（B）Professional] shoplifters / usually steal expensive items.
2. If caught, / [（A）compulsive　（B）professional] shoplifters usually feel guilty.
3. Teenagers often shoplift / because they [（A）need the items they shoplift　（B）enjoy the thrill of stealing].

Reading ②

1. Holidays are stressful for kleptomaniacs / because they fear [（A）committing a crime　（B）being mugged].
2. According to Terry, / kleptomaniacs cannot live without [（A）stealing　（B）working].
3. Most people come to CASA / because they [（A）have been told by the judge　（B）want to change themselves].

Reading-based Writing

(a) 本文の表現を使って次の日本語を英語にしましょう。
(b) 音声で正解を確認したら音読しましょう。
(c) ペアワーク：Aさんが日本語を読み、Bさんは何も見ずに英語を言いましょう。

Reading ①

(1) 強迫的万引き犯は捕まると、泣いて恥を感じるかもしれない。

　　If ＿＿＿＿＿＿＿＿＿＿＿＿＿＿＿＿, they ＿＿＿＿＿＿＿＿＿＿＿＿＿＿＿＿.

(2) 警察が職業的万引き犯を捕まえると、彼らは逃げようとする。

　　If ＿＿＿＿＿＿＿＿＿＿＿＿＿＿＿＿, they ＿＿＿＿＿＿＿＿＿＿＿＿＿＿＿＿.

(3) 貧乏な人たちは普通、食品、赤ん坊のおむつ、洗面用品などの必需品を盗む。

　　The poor ＿＿＿＿＿＿＿＿＿＿＿＿＿＿＿＿＿＿＿＿＿＿＿＿＿＿＿＿.

Reading ②

(4) 彼らは盗むことに強迫的欲求があるため買い物に行くのが怖い。

They are _____.

(5) 彼の中毒はあまりにひどくなり、毎日何かを盗んだ。

His _____.

(6) このグループにやってくる人のほとんどは、毎日を乗り切るための方法として万引きをするのだ。

Most of _____.

Speeded Vocab Production

(a) 英単語を音声の後について発音してみましょう。
(b) 日本語だけを見ながら、すべての英単語が60秒以内（最終的には30秒以内）に言えるよう練習しましょう。
(c) ペアワーク：Aさんが日本語をランダムな順番で読み、Bさんは英語を即座に言いましょう。

万引き	強制・強迫	やましく感じる	スリルを求める人	認める
値札	恥	必需品	中毒患者	匿名の
やめられない	感情	おしめ	衝動的な	〜を乗り切る

shoplifting	compulsion	feel guilty	thrill seeker	admit
price tag	shame	necessities	(n) addict	anonymous
compulsive	emotion	diaper	impulsive	cope with〜

Definition-based Vocab Work

(a) 上の語群の中から、次の定義に当たる語を選びましょう。
(b) ペアワーク：Aさんがランダムに定義を読み、Bさんは該当する単語を言いましょう。
(c) ペアワーク：Aさんが単語とその定義を読み、Bさんは何も見ずに繰り返しましょう。

1. [　　　　] = one's name not being made public
2. [　　　　] = a strong feeling such as love, hate, or anger
3. [　　　　] = a piece of soft cloth put between a baby's legs
4. [　　　　] = a person who is unable to stop taking harmful drugs

Unit 11 | Shoplifting : Why is the price tag still on your hat?

Idea Exchange ☞

(a) 下の質問にどう答えるか考えましょう。
(b) ペアワーク：それぞれの質問に対する答えをお互いに紹介しながら、話し合ってみましょう。
(c) 論点をひとつに絞って話して（または書いて）みましょう。

1. Honestly, have you ever been tempted to shoplift?

2. Do you think shoplifting is a big problem in Japan? Why or why not?

3. If people shoplift, why do they do it?

4. Do you know of someone who has shoplifted or who is often shoplifting?

5. Have you ever seen anyone shoplift? If so, what did you do?

6. Which of these solutions are probably effective for reducing the problem of shoplifting? Which of them are probably not effective? Why?
   - More security guards
   - More cameras
   - Stricter laws
   - Education
   - Therapy
   - Government help for the poor

7. How can teachers help stop shoplifting?

8. How can parents help stop shoplifting?

9. How can the government help stop shoplifting?

10. If you got to know that a friend of yours was habitually shoplifting, what would you do?

Unit 12

Drug Trends

Legal but lethal

Reading 1 Legal Drugs and Teenagers

Tobacco
Tobacco is the most common and dangerous legal drug. Long-term use causes serious diseases such as heart disease and lung cancer. Almost 25 percent of young teenagers smoke regularly. In addition, 85 percent of teenagers who smoke become addicted.

Alcohol
Alcohol is a depressant that can affect people in many different ways. Some people are relaxed by the drug. Others lose their inhibitions completely so they do stupid, and sometimes dangerous, things. Some people become alcoholics. Alcohol addiction destroys the lives of millions of people every year. Alcohol is illegal for teenagers, but they are drinking more than ever.

Inhalants
Inhalants are drugs that you can inhale to get high. Inhaling, or sniffing, is very popular with very young teenagers because the products are easy to find. Common household products such as nail polish remover, spray paints, and cleaning fluids are sniffable. Inhalants can cause brain damage and even death.   (147 words)

Reading 2 The World's Most Popular Drug

Caffeine is one of the most popular drugs in the world. Ninety percent of Americans consume it every single day. It is found in coffee, tea, cola, chocolate, and a variety of other things.

Most people don't realize it is an addictive drug. It stimulates the brain in the same way as illegal drugs such as cocaine and heroin do. Although caffeine is not as strong as these drugs, it is still addictive. If you must have caffeine every day, you are addicted.

Caffeine does not have the same effect on everyone. While some people can have three caffeine drinks in an hour and be fine, others may feel nervous and jumpy after just one drink.

Caffeine has some medical uses. Doctors use it as a heart stimulant. But most people take it when they feel tired and need energy. They don't realize that they are hurting themselves. When the body is tired, it needs rest. Caffeine stops it from resting.   (161 words)

Outline Reproduction

(a) まず英文の内容に合う選択肢を選び、音声で正解を確認しましょう。
(b) スラッシュ（/）で区切られたチャンク毎に覚えて言う練習をしましょう。
(c) ペアワーク：Aさんが正答あるいは誤答の選択肢を用いた文を音読し、Bさんはそれを聞いてTrueかFalseかを言いましょう。

Reading ①

1. Tobacco is / the most common and dangerous drug / [(A) legal (B) illegal] for adults.
2. Alcohol is a drug / that has [(A) different effects on different people (B) the same effect on almost everyone].
3. If you use inhalants, / you will feel [(A) high (B) low] / but may lose your life later.

Reading ②

1. Most people do not realize / that caffeine contained in coffee and tea is [(A) illegal (B) addictive].
2. Caffeine [(A) has (B) does not have] the same effect / on everyone.
3. Caffeine may make you feel less tired / [(A) and it does (B) but it does not] actually give you energy.

Reading-based Writing

(a) 本文の表現を使って次の日本語を英語にしましょう。
(b) 音声で正解を確認したら音読しましょう。
(c) ペアワーク：Aさんが日本語を読み、Bさんは何も見ずに英語を言いましょう。

Reading ①

(1) 長期にわたる喫煙は心臓病や肺がんといった深刻な疾病の原因となる。

　　Long-term _____.

(2) 人によっては完全に抑制を失くし、ばかなことをする。

　　Some people _____.

(3) 吸入物は脳障害を引き起こし、死の原因となることさえある。

　　Inhalants _____.

Reading ②

(4) アメリカ人の9割は毎日カフェインを消費する。

　　Ninety percent _____.

(5) カフェインは、コカインやヘロインと同じ仕方で脳を刺激する。

　　Caffeine _____.

(6) ほとんどの人は疲れを感じエネルギーが必要な時にカフェインを摂取する。

　　Most people _____.

Speeded Vocab Production

(a) 英単語を音声の後について発音してみましょう。
(b) 日本語だけを見ながら、すべての英単語が60秒以内（最終的には30秒以内）に言えるよう練習しましょう。
(c) ペアワーク：Aさんが日本語をランダムな順番で読み、Bさんは英語を即座に言いましょう。

長期的な	鎮静剤	完全に	液体	効果
病気	影響する・作用する	アルコール中毒患者	中毒性がある	医学的な
規則的に・習慣的に	抑制・禁止	吸い込む	不安で、興奮して	興奮剤・刺激剤

long-term	depressant	completely	fluid	effect
disease	affect	(n) alcoholic	addictive	medical
regularly	inhibition	inhale	nervous	stimulant

Definition-based Vocab Work

(a) 上の語群の中から、次の定義に当たる語を選びましょう。
(b) ペアワーク：Aさんがランダムに定義を読み、Bさんは該当する単語を言いましょう。
(c) ペアワーク：Aさんが単語とその定義を読み、Bさんは何も見ずに繰り返しましょう。

1. [　　　　　] = a drug that makes you feel more relaxed and sleepy
2. [　　　　　] = a person who cannot stop drinking alcohol
3. [　　　　　] = a change that something causes in something else or someone
4. [　　　　　] = a drug that makes you feel full of energy

Idea Exchange 👉

（a）下の質問にどう答えるか考えましょう。
（b）ペアワーク：それぞれの質問に対する答えをお互いに紹介しながら、話し合ってみましょう。
（c）論点をひとつに絞って話して（または書いて）みましょう。

1. Which of these drugs should the government control?
    a) tobacco
    b) alcohol
    c) marihuana
    d) cocaine
    e) inhalants
    f) caffeine

2. How should they control each one?
    a) Make it illegal for anyone to have it.
    b) Make it illegal for anyone to sell it.
    c) Make it illegal for people under 18 to have or to sell it.
    d) Tax the users.
    e) Tax the companies that produce it.
    f) Educate the public about it.
    g) Have free treatment programs for addicts.

3. Do you agree or disagree with the following statement?
    "Drug use is a victimless crime. Drug users are only hurting themselves. Also, when drugs are illegal, the price of drugs goes up. As a result of this price, crime increases and hurts everyone. For these two reasons, drugs should be legal."

Unit 13

Nature

Paradise lost—Can we get it back?

Reading 1 The Story of Bikini

After World War II, the American government wanted to test nuclear bombs. The government needed to find a place far away from civilization. They chose the tiny island of Bikini in the Pacific Ocean. Bikini was far from sea and air routes, and the U.S. government controlled it.

05 In order to get permission to test the bomb, the American governor of Bikini went to talk to the people who lived on Bikini. There were only 167. He explained that the tests were for "the good of mankind and could end all world wars." He also said that the islanders could return after the tests were finished. In the end, the Bikinians agreed.

10 Unfortunately, nuclear scientists were wrong about the strength of the bomb. The bomb was 1,000 times stronger than the bombs that destroyed Hiroshima and Nagasaki in Japan. It caused much more dangerous radiation than they expected. Now, more than 50 years after the nuclear test, the Bikinians are still living in exile. (162 words)

Reading 2 Here Today, Gone Tomorrow

Tashkent, Uzbekistan—The Aral Sea began getting smaller in the 1960s. At that time, the former Soviet government started a large irrigation project. They used water from the Amu Darya River and the Syr Darya River to irrigate crops. From 1960 to 1990, the area of irrigated land in

05 Central Asia more than doubled. Cotton production also increased. Soon the region was the world's fourth largest cotton producer.

Unfortunately, there were some very bad results. With less water, the sea started to become smaller. Within decades it was 50 percent smaller. The water in the Aral Sea is now very salty. Most of the native plants and

10 animals cannot live in such salty water. In addition, a lot of the drinking water is very salty. The salt has caused increases in kidney disease, diarrhea, and other serious health problems. In short, a place that used to be a successful farming and fishing area is now becoming an environmental wasteland. (157 words)

Outline Reproduction

(a) まず英文の内容に合う選択肢を選び、音声で正解を確認しましょう。
(b) スラッシュ（/）で区切られたチャンク毎に覚えて言う練習をしましょう。
(c) ペアワーク：Aさんが正答あるいは誤答の選択肢を用いた文を音読し、Bさんはそれを聞いてTrueかFalseかを言いましょう。

Reading ①

1. The American government chose Bikini / because it was [(A) far from (B) close to] civilization.
2. The people in Bikini believed / that they would [(A) never be (B) be] able to return to the island / after the tests.
3. The bombs tested were stronger than expected / and [(A) destroyed (B) improved] the environment of Bikini.

Reading ②

1. The Aral Sea began to get smaller / as the area of irrigated land became [(A) smaller (B) larger].
2. Native animals and plants have disappeared / because the water is [(A) too salty (B) not salty enough].
3. The drinking water around the Sea is very salty, / which caused health [(A) problems (B) benefits] among people.

Reading-based Writing

(a) 本文の表現を使って次の日本語を英語にしましょう。
(b) 音声で正解を確認したら音読しましょう。
(c) ペアワーク：Aさんが日本語を読み、Bさんは何も見ずに英語を言いましょう。

Reading ①

(1) 第二次世界大戦後、アメリカ政府は核爆弾をテストしたいと思っていた。

After _____, _____.

(2) 彼はそのテストは「人類の幸福のためであり、すべての世界大戦を終わらせることができる」と説明した。

He _____.

(3) 不幸なことに、核科学者たちはその爆弾の威力に関して誤っていた。

Unfortunately, _____.

Reading ②

(4) 彼らは川の水を利用して、穀物を灌漑した。

They _____.

(5) 灌漑用地の面積は2倍以上になり、綿花の生産量は増えた。

The _____.

(6) かつて豊かな農地だった場所はいまや環境的には荒れ地となりつつある。

A place _____.

Speeded Vocab Production

(a) 英単語を音声の後について発音してみましょう。
(b) 日本語だけを見ながら、すべての英単語が60秒以内（最終的には30秒以内）に言えるよう練習しましょう。
(c) ペアワーク：Aさんが日本語をランダムな順番で読み、Bさんは英語を即座に言いましょう。

核爆弾	人類	流浪の身で	作物	腎臓
文明	力	地域に固有の	地域	下痢
許可	放射能	灌漑（かんがい）	10年	荒れ地

nuclear bomb	mankind	in exile	crops	kidney
civilization	strength	native	region	diarrhea
permission	radiation	irrigation	decade	wasteland

Definition-based Vocab Work

(a) 上の語群の中から、次の定義に当たる語を選びましょう。
(b) ペアワーク：Aさんがランダムに定義を読み、Bさんは該当する単語を言いましょう。
(c) ペアワーク：Aさんが単語とその定義を読み、Bさんは何も見ずに繰り返しましょう。

1. [   ] = the act of allowing someone to do something
2. [   ] = giving water to an area of land where crops grow
3. [   ] = plants grown by farmers and used as food
4. [   ] = an illness in which waste from the bowel is watery

Idea Exchange

(a) 下の質問にどう答えるか考えましょう。
(b) ペアワーク：それぞれの質問に対する答えをお互いに紹介しながら、話し合ってみましょう。
(c) 論点をひとつに絞って話して（または書いて）みましょう。

1. Should governments be responsible for fixing the environmental problems they cause? Why or why not?

2. Do governments today make these same kinds of mistakes? Why or why not?

3. How big a problem is the environment? Why?

4. How responsible is each of the groups below for environmental problems? Why or why not?
    a) ordinary citizens in developed countries
    b) leaders of corporations
    c) officials in governments
    d) scientists such as geologists
    e) ordinary citizens in developing countries

5. How can each group help to solve these environmental problems?

Unit 14

White-Collar Crime

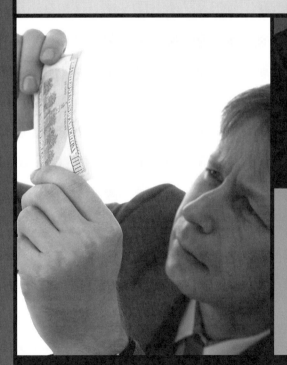

When *A LOT* just isn't enough!

Reading 1 What Is White-Collar Crime?

Sociologist Edwin Sutherland was the first person to use the term *white-collar crime*. Sutherland used the phrase white-collar because most of the criminals that he studied were white-collar workers—people with occupations that don't require manual labor. These included business people, government workers, doctors, and lawyers. He compared white-collar crime with street crime. In one basic way these criminals are the same—people commit these crimes for money. However, they are different in another important way. Street crime is often physically violent. White-collar criminals usually hurt people's finances, but they don't often hit them.

Before Sutherland, sociologists believed that poverty was the cause of most crime; they thought that people committed crimes because they were poor. Sutherland argued that wealthy people were often criminals, too. They weren't poor. They were just greedy. They were people who had a lot, but wanted more. Sutherland also believed that white-collar crime was more dangerous than street crime, even though it was nonviolent. Why? Because it made people distrust important social institutions such as government and business organizations. (172 words)

Reading 2 What Do White-Collar Criminals Do?

White-collar criminals commit the following crimes:
- Fraud: Getting money by "selling" products or services that do not actually exist.
- Embezzlement: Taking money or property that the white-collar criminal controls but does not own.
- Bribery: Giving a government worker or company employee a gift so that the person will help the criminal.
- Forgery: Signing another person's name to a check or other legal paper.
- Insider Trading: Using information that the public doesn't know in order to decide to buy or sell stock.
- Kickback: Similar to a bribe. Giving money back to the person who purchased your service or product; this money profits the buyer, not the buyer's business.
- Money Laundering: Investing money from an illegal business (dirty money) in a legal business to cover or hide criminal activity.

(134 words)

Unit 14 | White-collar crime : When *A LOT* just isn't enough!

Outline Reproduction

(a) まず英文の内容に合う選択肢を選び、音声で正解を確認しましょう。
(b) スラッシュ（/）で区切られたチャンク毎に覚えて言う練習をしましょう。
(c) ペアワーク：Aさんが正答あるいは誤答の選択肢を用いた文を音読し、Bさんはそれを聞いてTrueかFalseかを言いましょう。

Reading 1

1. White-collar crimes are different from street crimes / in that they usually [(A) do not involve (B) involve] physical violence.
2. The cause of white-collar crimes / is [(A) greed, rather than poverty (B) poverty, rather than greed].
3. In a sense, / while-collar crimes are more harmful than street crimes / because they [(A) damage (B) enhance] people's trust in social institutions.

Reading 2

1. Fraud means / getting money by "selling" products or services / that [(A) do not actually (B) actually] exist.
2. Bribery means / giving a gift to someone with power / so that the person will help you [(A) secretly (B) publicly].
3. If you sign another person's name to a legal paper, / you have committed [(A) forgery (B) embezzlement].

Reading-based Writing

(a) 本文の表現を使って次の日本語を英語にしましょう。
(b) 音声で正解を確認したら音読しましょう。
(c) ペアワーク：Aさんが日本語を読み、Bさんは何も見ずに英語を言いましょう。

Reading 1

(1) ホワイトカラー労働者とは、肉体労働が不要な職業の人々だ。

　　 White-collar workers _____.

(2) ある基本的な点においてこれらの犯罪者は同じ――金のために犯罪を犯す――である。

　　 In _____.

(3) 彼らは多くを持っていたが、さらに多くを欲しがった人々だった。

　　 They _____.

Reading ②

(4) 自分で扱ってはいるが自分のものではない金銭を自分のものにすれば、それは横領である。

　　If _____, that _____.

(5) 株の売買の決断を、一般人が知らない情報を使って行えば、それはインサイダー取引である。

　　If _____, that _____.

(6) 非合法な商売で得た金銭を、合法的な商売に投資することで犯罪的活動を隠せば、それはマネーロンダリングである。

　　If _____, that _____.

Speeded Vocab Production

(a) 英単語を音声の後について発音してみましょう。
(b) 日本語だけを見ながら、すべての英単語が60秒以内（最終的には30秒以内）に言えるよう練習しましょう。
(c) ペアワーク：Aさんが日本語をランダムな順番で読み、Bさんは英語を即座に言いましょう。

犯罪	肉体労働	貧困	怪しむ	横領
犯罪者	財政状態	富裕な	機構、組織	贈賄
職業	社会学者	欲深い	詐欺行為	偽造

crime	manual labor	poverty	(v) distrust	embezzlement
criminal	finance	wealthy	institution	bribery
occupation	sociologist	greedy	fraud	forgery

Definition-based Vocab Work

(a) 上の語群の中から、次の定義に当たる語を選びましょう。
(b) ペアワーク：Aさんがランダムに定義を読み、Bさんは該当する単語を言いましょう。
(c) ペアワーク：Aさんが単語とその定義を読み、Bさんは何も見ずに繰り返しましょう。

1. [　　　　　] = someone who does something illegal
2. [　　　　　] = work done using your hands rather than your mind
3. [　　　　　] = a person who scientifically studies about society
4. [　　　　　] = a large organization that has a particular purpose

Idea Exchange

(a) 下の質問にどう答えるか考えましょう。
(b) ペアワーク：それぞれの質問に対する答えをお互いに紹介しながら、話し合ってみましょう。
(c) 論点をひとつに絞って話して（または書いて）みましょう。

1. Do you agree with Sutherland (referred to in Reading 1) that white-collar crimes are more dangerous to society than street crimes?

2. Which types of white-collar crimes do you think are the most frequent?

3. How big a problem is white-collar crime?

4. Should white-collar criminals go to jail like street criminals or should they be made to pay a lot of money instead?

5. Would you ever cheat on your taxes?

6. Would you ever sell a car with a minor problem and not tell the buyer?

7. Would you ever sell a car with a serious problem and not tell the buyer?

8. Would you ever sell an item with a minor problem at the Yahoo Auction and not tell the buyer?

9. Would you take something from your university that is worth less than ¥500, like a toilet paper roll in a toilet?

10. When employed in the future, would you take something from your employer that is worth more than ¥10,000?

Unit 15

Vocabulary & Sentence Structure Review

これまで学習した語彙を復習しましょう。

Part ① 以下の定義に当てはまる語を言い／書きましょう。

1. [　　　　　] = a person who cannot stop drinking alcohol
2. [　　　　　] = a group of people with the same interests
3. [　　　　　] = someone who has power in an organization
4. [　　　　　] = what you like and prefer
5. [　　　　　] = a thing that helps you to be better than other people
6. [　　　　　] = one's name not being made public
7. [　　　　　] = a reason somebody uses to show something is true
8. [　　　　　] = a group of people watching or listening to a performance
9. [　　　　　] = the conditions of a person's life
10. [　　　　　] = an animal produced from the cells of another animal
11. [　　　　　] = the feeling that you have a high ability
12. [　　　　　] = someone who has entered a contest
13. [　　　　　] = someone who does something illegal
14. [　　　　　] = plants grown by farmers and used as food
15. [　　　　　] = a circle put on the head of someone who has won a contest
16. [　　　　　] = a phrase that says exactly what a word means
17. [　　　　　] = a drug that makes you feel more relaxed and sleepy
18. [　　　　　] = a machine or tool for a specific purpose
19. [　　　　　] = a disease in which there is too much sugar in your blood
20. [　　　　　] = an illness in which waste from the bowel is watery
21. [　　　　　] = a change that something causes in something else or someone
22. [　　　　　] = a sudden serious and dangerous situation
23. [　　　　　] = two or more groups that have joined together to form a larger group
24. [　　　　　] = mathematical relationship expressed in symbols
25. [　　　　　] = how fast your heart is beating
26. [　　　　　] = someone who copies the way other people speak or behave
27. [　　　　　] = a large organization that has a particular purpose
28. [　　　　　] = good at learning and understanding about things
29. [　　　　　] = a person who examines crimes
30. [　　　　　] = giving water to an area of land where crops grow
31. [　　　　　] = a room or building used for scientific research
32. [　　　　　] = clothes that need to be washed
33. [　　　　　] = a machine with blades for cutting grass
34. [　　　　　] = allowed by law
35. [　　　　　] = work done using your hands rather than your mind

36. [   ] = your feelings or thoughts about something
37. [   ] = a gas that is in the air and is necessary for us to live
38. [   ] = the act of allowing someone to do something
39. [   ] = a person who buys things for personal use
40. [   ] = all members of a group of people living in a place
41. [   ] = someone who earns money by having sex with people
42. [   ] = someone whose job is to research how people think and feel
43. [   ] = what you do something for
44. [   ] = what you do as a result of something that has happened
45. [   ] = someone whose business is selling houses or land for building
46. [   ] = someone whose job is to study and investigate a subject
47. [   ] = a complete change in ways of thinking or behaving
48. [   ] = always sitting down and not moving enough
49. [   ] = a building that gives a place to stay for people without home
50. [   ] = a person who scientifically studies about society
51. [   ] = a drug that makes you feel full of energy
52. [   ] = two children born at the same time to the same mother
53. [   ] = a place where an organized event takes place

Part ② 以下の日本語に対応する英語を言いましょう。

Xの味付けをした	大切な	クローン	遺伝子の	最愛の
ばかげた	同じに	創りだす	最近亡くなった	気持ちを動転させるような
ばかげた	双子	実験室	決定	知的な

思い出に残る	華々しい	合法的な	不動産業者	売春婦
安価な	モノマネ芸人	報酬がよい	〜に手を染める	さわるな！
ろうそくに照らされた	大気圏外の宇宙空間	経験豊かな	売春行為	めったに〜ない

状況	児童福祉	結局は	手頃な値段の	職員
離婚する	養子を迎えている家族	非合法の	避難所	解決策
拒む	信じがたいほど	寝泊まり	緊急事態	ビンタ

成果	自慢する	不利であること	酸素	公平な機会
覆い隠す	得意そうに話す	刺激する	主張	統制が効かなくなる
自信	有利であること	減少させる	環境	続ける

利益	目的	団体	詐欺	人口
稼ぐ	困窮している	ピラミッド	参加	捜査員
保証する	～から成っている	完結して	全体の	不幸にして

公式	研究者	反応	くるくる回す	組織する・企画する
予測する	脈拍数	負の	局、省	必死な
島国	顔の	義理の母親	大卒の資格	発展

混乱している	心理学者	機会	～を目指して競う	ポーズを取る
勇敢に	心理的な	外見	出場者	競争
冠、頭飾り	派手なショー	例外	観客	全体的な

血圧	座ってばかりいる	装置	食べ過ぎている	飢えている
糖尿病	芝刈り機	脂肪	研究所	見なされる
肥満した	省力のための	十分に食べていない	～と等しい	過度の

やみつきである	金銭状態・資金力	死の床	必要である	革命
舞台・会	熟考・意見	可能性が高い	やりとり、会話	満足
嗜好・好み	消費者	経験	促す	資本主義のしくみ

タイミングを一致させた	生活のために	シワのよった	連邦・連盟	決める
絶対に	定義	洗濯物	競争的な	意見
組み合わせる	極端な	位置・場所	体操	競技者

万引き	強制	やましく感じる	スリルを求める人	認める
値札	恥	必需品	中毒患者	匿名の
やめられない	感情	おしめ	衝動的な	～を乗り切る

長期的な	鎮静剤	完全に	液体	効果
病気	影響する・作用する	アルコール中毒患者	中毒性がある	医学的な
規則的に・習慣的に	抑制・禁止	吸い込む	不安で、興奮して	興奮剤・刺激剤

核爆弾	人類	流浪の身で	作物	腎臓
文明	力	地域に固有の	地域	下痢
許可	放射能	灌漑（かんがい）	10年	荒れ地

犯罪	肉体労働	貧困	怪しむ	使い込み
犯罪者	金回り、財政状態	富裕な	機構、組織	贈賄
職業	社会学者	欲深い	詐欺行為	偽造

Part ③ Invisible-gap Filling

以下はすべて Unit 1 〜 Unit 14 の本文のどこかに出てきた文（または文章）ですが、それぞれ、単語が1語削除されています（短縮形も1語扱い）。文のどの位置から、何という単語が削除されているかを考えましょう。（文の構造および意味が分かれば、削除された単語も分かるようになっています。）答えがわかったら、自分で Unit 1 〜 Unit 14 の本文のなかで該当する文を探して、答え合わせをしてください。できるかぎり速く探すことが、スキャニングの練習になります。

1) Alcohol is a depressant can affect people in many different ways.
2) Although athletes know that working hard is the way to win, they also know that drugs can give them a special.
3) An activity is not a sport a judge or a group of judges chooses the winner.
4) Being overweight can serious health problems such as heart disease, high blood pressure, and diabetes.
5) But while one woman waits for a clone, others are looking for new pets. Karen and Michael Lawrence decided to spend $50 of $50,000. When their cat, Marshall, died, they went to the animal shelter.
6) In order to permission to test the bomb, the American governor of Bikini went to talk to the people who lived on Bikini.
7) In short, a place used to be a successful farming and fishing area is now becoming an environmental wasteland.
8) Insider Trading: Using information that the public know in order to decide to buy or sell stock.
9) Liz refused to go into the child welfare system because she didn't want to with strangers in a foster family or a group home.
10) Most cultures consider a man's appearance as important as a woman's.
11) Most people believe that sports must combine physical activity

competition.
12) She eventually earned a scholarship and, in 2000, she Harvard.
13) Sociologists believed that poverty was the cause of most crime; they thought that people crimes because they were poor.
14) Some child psychologists say that the contests have many disadvantages than advantages.
15) Some people ask, "What's wrong with athletes using drugs to help them better?"
16) The addictive-compulsive shoplifter, like myself and most of the people who come to the group, as a way to cope with life," Schulman says.
17) The company expects to make a lot of cloning pets after they die.
18) The consumerist environment we live encourages us to have packaged experiences.
19) The government of the tiny island nation of Singapore is spending money marriage.
20) They believe shoplifting is necessary to support and their families.
21) Though some people say, "Dog restaurants are absurd," dog owner Sherry Evans agree.
22) Two researchers at the University of Washington created a mathematical that predicts divorce.
23) Unfortunately, the number of overweight people is increasing faster than the starvation rate is.
24) We ask city officials to focus on positive solutions—increased housing and services that will help people get the street.
25) We usually call these machines labor-saving devices. Maybe if we called them fat-development devices, people would using them.
26) While some people can have three caffeine drinks in an hour and be, others may feel nervous and jumpy after just one drink.
27) Women think it is safe because they believe women hurt other women.

JPCA
日本出版著作権協会
http://www.e-jpca.com/

本書は日本出版著作権協会（JPCA）が委託管理する著作物です。複写（コピー）・複製、その他著作物の利用については、事前にJPCA（電話03-3812-9424, e-mail:info@e-jpca.com）の許諾を得て下さい。なお、無断でコピー・スキャン・デジタル化等の複製をすることは著作権法上の例外を除き、著作権法違反となります。

Burning Issues
Pre-Intermediate Level

2015年4月10日　初版第1刷発行

著　者　Cheryl Pavlik
編著者　靜 哲人

発行者　森　信久
発行所　株式会社　松 柏 社
　　　　〒102-0072　東京都千代田区飯田橋1-6-1
　　　　TEL 03 (3230) 4813（代表）
　　　　FAX 03 (3230) 4857
　　　　http://www.shohakusha.com
　　　　e-mail: info@shohakusha.com

装　幀　小島トシノブ（NONdesign）
レイアウト組版・印刷・製本　美研プリンティング株式会社

略号＝693
ISBN978-4-88198-693-6
Copyright © 2015 by SHIZUKA Tetsuhito

本書を無断で複写・複製することを禁じます。
落丁・乱丁は送料小社負担にてお取り替え致します。

Series of Graded Readers
Burning Issues

Cheryl Pavlik 著　靜 哲人 編著

普遍的な題材と、一つのテーマについて複数のパッセージを設けた立体的な本文構成で定評のある人気のレベル別リーディングコースブックを日本で使いやすいよう徹底的に編纂！

Pre-Intermediate Level　　Intermediate Level　　Advanced Level

Exercises
◆本文内容確認のための正答選択問題　　◆日本語に合う英文を本文中から探して書き写す問題
◆語彙問題　　◆本文を読んで考えたことを自分の英語で語る・書く問題

□Pre-Intermediate／Intermediate各巻15章構成／Advanced14章構成

しょうはくしゃ　検索

www.shohakusha.com

Series of Graded Readers
CONNECTION

Milada Broukal 著

Starter's Level　　Pre-Intermediate Level　　Intermediate Level　　Advanced Level

ロングセラー Weaving It Together シリーズのリーディングセクションが装い新たに 15 章構成で刊行スタート！

タイの習慣、睡眠、スポーツ選手、笑いの効果、芸術など、アジア各国や欧米の面白く普遍的なテーマを扱った、グレード別リーディングコースブックの登場！

=== Exercises ===

◆提示された英文が本文の内容を正しく示しているかを問う T or F 問題
◆本文の内容の理解を問う問題　◆本文中の重要語彙を別の文脈で穴埋めする問題
◆本文の内容を示すセンテンスの誤りを見つける問題　他

□各巻 15 章構成